Zoo dos you can do!

Compiled by Amy E. Sklansky

Little, Brown and Company
Boston   New York   London

First Edition

ZOOM, ZOOMer, ZOOMguest, ZOOMsci, ZOOMchat, ZOOMgames, ZOOMzone, ZOOMjournal, ZOOMdo, ZOOMparty, Zoops, Zoinks!, whatZup!, CafeZOOM, ZOOMzingers, ZOOMfun, ZOOMerang, ZOOMa Cum Laude, ZOOMmedia, Ubbi Dubbi, Zfact, Zmail, ZOOMkids, By Kids, For Kids, Fannee Doolee, and other composite ZOOM marks contained herein are trademarks of the WGBH Educational Foundation. Zoinks!™ compiled by Bill Shribman.

ISBN 0-316-95276-1
Library of Congress Catalog Card Number 00-130081

10 9 8 7 6 5 4 3 2 1

Q-KPT

Printed in the United States of America

Hacky Sack is a registered trademark of Mattel, Inc. All brand-name products mentioned herein are trademarks of their respective owners.

Funding for ZOOM is provided by
public television viewers,
the National Science Foundation,
and the Corporation for Public Broadcasting.

Design by WGBH Design

Photo credits: copyright page: Mark Ostow; pages 2–3: Mark Ostow; page 4: Mark Ostow; page 9: Lisa Abitbol; page 12: Lisa Abitbol; page 13: Mark Ostow; page 16: Lisa Abitbol; page 36: Lisa Abitbol; page 49: Mark Ostow; page 51: Mark Ostow; page 56: Lisa Abitbol; page 57: Lisa Abitbol, Mark Ostow; page 58: Lisa Abitbol; page 59: Mark Ostow; page 60: Mark Ostow, Bill Shribman; page 61: Bill Shribman, Steve Offsey.

Illustration credits: page 13: Steve Schudlich; page 16: Amity Femia; page 19: Amity Femia; page 20: Amity Femia; page 22: Steve Schudlich; page 24: Steve Schudlich; page 26–27: Steve Schudlich; page 30–31: Amity Femia; page 32: Amity Femia; page 34–35: Steve Schudlich; page 39: Steve Schudlich; page 47: Amity Femia; page 56: Amity Femia.

Hey ZOOMers,

ZOOM is TV by kids, for kids. **Without you,** there wouldn't be a show! Everything you see on ZOOM was sent in by kids from all over the country.

Each show is a **cool mix** of games, experiments, crafts, kid guests, recipes, brainteasers, jokes, skits, and more. After watching, you'll want to try them all yourself.

But ZOOM is more than TV. We have a Web site at **pbskids.org/zoom** and our own newsletter called ZOOMerang. So check us out when you're surfing the Internet. Send us your ideas by mail or e-mail, and we'll send you the latest edition of ZOOMerang and consider putting your ideas on the show or our site.

Do you like to **craft, build,** or **bake** things? In this book you'll discover our top picks from the show — from funny fridge magnets to a breezy balloon car to one-of-a-kind cupcake cones. Plus we've added some brand-new stuff you'll want to try. You can do anything if you set your mind to it.

You can ZOOMdo it!

P.S. **Check out** the last page to find out how to send your ideas to ZOOM.

1

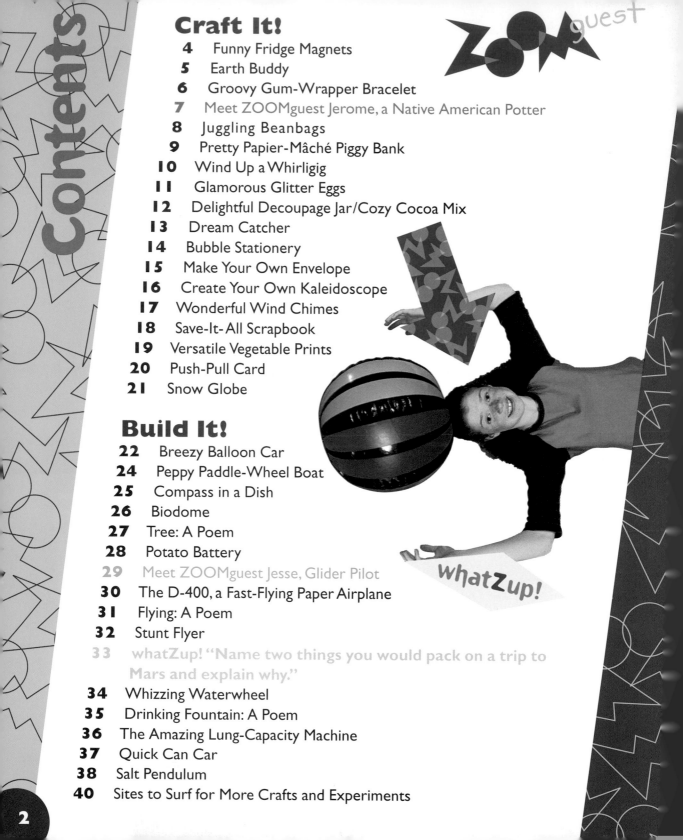

Contents

Craft It!

Build It!

Bake It!

Café ZOOM

> What? You can't understand what he's saying? That's because he's speaking Ubbi Dubbi, ZOOM's secret language. We promise to reveal the secret to speaking Ubbi Dubbi before this book ends — so keep reading!

Everything You Always Wanted to Know About ZOOM

> Hubey, dubo yubou lubike to crubaft, bubuild, uband bubake thubings? Thuben thubis ubis thube bubook fubor yubou!

E-mailed by Amy M. of Ellicott City, Maryland, and Lara and Jack W. of Wellesley, Massachusetts.

Funny Fridge Magnets

"They're loads of laughs and make great keepsakes." — Amy M.

Feel like a giggle? Need a laugh? Make some Funny Fridge Magnets by gluing photos of people's heads to bodies cut out of magazines.

You will need:

- photos of family, friends, and pets (Make sure you have permission to cut these up!)
- old magazines
- scissors
- glue
- thin cardboard (like the back of a pad of paper)
- magnets (You can find these at an office supply store.)

Cut just the face out of a photo. **Look** through magazines until you **find** a body that looks funny with the face on top of it. **Cut** out the body. (Wait until later to trim it carefully.) **Glue** the body and head to a piece of cardboard. Then cut away the cardboard around the figure, **trimming** the figure more closely if needed. **Glue** a magnet to the back of the figure. Let your Funny Fridge Magnet **dry** before sticking it on your fridge or giving it to a friend.

P.S. Instead of making magnets, you could also make funny pictures by pasting the figures onto a scene you cut out or draw yourself.

Here's a joke from Latisha J. of Baton Rouge, Louisiana:

What did the mayonnaise say to the refrigerator?

Answer: Close the door, I'm dressing.

Sent in by Rachel K. of Spring Green, Wisconsin; Lauren and Elise T. of Winchester, Massachusetts; and Merve K. of Windsor, Ontario.

Earth Buddy

Make friends with an Earth Buddy and give it a grass haircut.

You will need:

- old nylon stocking
- scissors
- 2 tablespoons grass seed
- sawdust
- a few rubber bands
- saucer
- markers or thumbtacks
- googly eyes from a craft store (optional)

Rachel K. e-mailed: "These bags o' sawdust make great pets, uh, plants."

Cut the foot off the stocking. Pour the grass seed into the toe. **Fill** the rest of the foot with sawdust. **Tie** the top with a rubber band. **Turn** it upside down and place it toe up on a saucer. **Squeeze** it into a nice-looking head. **Add** eyes, nose, and mouth with markers or thumbtacks. If you have googly eyes, glue them on. Use your fingers to **pinch** and mold a nose for your Buddy.

Then **tie** off the nose with a rubber band. **Soak** your Buddy with water and place it in a sunny spot. **Water** it a little every day. When its hair gets long enough, give it a trim — maybe a flattop?

P.S. Make another Earth Buddy to keep yours company. You could give them different features, haircuts, and even accessories!

Zfact:

Talking to your plants may actually help them grow better. However, it's less what you're saying and more what you're breathing as you speak. Plants like the carbon dioxide and moisture you breathe out when you talk! So have a chat with your Earth Buddy and see what happens....

5

Groovy Gum-Wrapper Bracelet

You can chew your gum and wear it, too. (Well, you can wear the wrappers anyhow.) Save the long, thin chewing gum wrappers until you have a nice collection. Then follow these easy steps:

"It's amazing to see how strong this gum-wrapper chain is!" — Katie K.

1 **Open** the printed wrapper and cut it in half the long way.

2 **Fold** one piece in half the long way so the printed part of the paper shows. **Fold** it in half the long way again.

3 Now **fold** in the two ends until they meet.

4 **Fold** one half inward to make a V. Each side of your V is a slot. **Make** another V with the other half of your wrapper. **Slide** the top ends of your new V all the way through the slots of your old V.

5 Continue **making** links until you have enough for a bracelet or necklace.

Z fact:

Bracelets have quite a history. In the **Stone Age,** bracelets were made of shells, bones, teeth, or claws. Bracelets have even been found in ancient **Egyptian tombs.** And Roman soldiers were often **rewarded** with **gold bracelets** for courage in battle.

Meet Jerome
A Native American Potter

Q: What is your name and where do you live?

Jerome: Some people know me as Jerome, but my family calls me Ajuano Hompi, which means "in the evening time." I live in Santa Clara Pueblo, New Mexico, where my ancestors have lived for five hundred years.

Q: How did you learn to make pottery?

Jerome: I started making pottery when I was six years old. My grandma taught me.

Q: What materials do you use?

Jerome: We mix sand in with clay because it makes the clay stronger. It takes a while to put the sand and clay together and your hands get tired. But it's fun.

Q: What do you do after the clay is ready?

Jerome: I make it into figures. Today I chose a turtle because it's very traditional to me and my people. I paint the turtle with red paint. After that, I have to go over it with old rocks so that it will look pretty and be shiny. The rocks I use to do this have been in my family for hundreds of years. I'm proud to use them now as my great-great-grandmothers used them a long time ago. After I spend hours and hours polishing it, then I make a design. The last thing I do is fire the turtle in an oven heated with cedar wood. We have to keep it in there for hours so it will dry just right. Then I paint the figure. I paint feathers on the turtle because feathers are used in traditional dances.

Q: Why do you make pottery?

Jerome: I think it's important to share my culture and my history and the way I do that is through making pottery.

Juggling Beanbags

Blow up a balloon and then let the air out. This will loosen up the balloon. **Fold** a piece of paper in half and then unfold it. Pour some beans on the paper and use it as a **funnel** to help you pour the beans into the bottle. Then **stretch** the balloon over the top of the bottle. Turn the bottle over so that all the beans **pour** into the balloon.

Blow up a second balloon and let the air out. Then cut off the top of the balloon and **stretch** it over the open end of the bean-filled balloon. **Repeat** this once more with the third balloon. There you have it—a juggling beanbag! Make two more and juggle away!

P.S. You can use one bag like a Hacky Sack.™

You will need:
- 3 balloons
- paper
- dried beans, such as lentils or split peas
- plastic soda bottle
- scissors

"One of my favorite games is Hacky Sack.™ One day I lost my favorite one, so I made my own. It works great!"
— Mandy G. of Lorain, Ohio

Pretty Papier-Mâché
Piggy Bank

You will need:

- masking tape
- 4 toilet paper tubes
- empty 2-liter soda bottle
- scissors
- small piece of cardboard
- 1½ cups flour
- 1½ cups water
- newspaper strips (1 or 2 inches wide)
- paint
- pipe cleaner

Save your pennies, nickels, dimes, and quarters for a rainy day in this Pretty Piggy Bank.

Tape the toilet paper tubes to 1 side of the soda bottle—these will be your pig's legs. **Cut** 2 triangles out of cardboard for the ears and tape them in place on the bottle.

Then **mix** flour and water until it looks like pancake batter. **Dip** a newspaper strip into the paste and squeeze off the excess paste by pulling the strip between 2 fingers. Then **lay** the strip on the bottle. Continue to do this, slightly overlapping each strip, until the entire pig and all its parts are covered. Then **repeat** twice so that there is a total of 3 layers of newspaper. Let the pig **dry** overnight.

Paint the pig any way you like—maybe pink or white with big black spots? **Curl** a pipe cleaner to make a tail. To finish your piggy bank, ask an adult to help you cut a slit in its back so you can drop in your coins.

Whubat duboes uban ubbi dubbi pubigguby bubank subay?

Uboink, uboink, ubof cubourse!

ent in by Christina C. of Rex, Georgia.

zfact

The world's **first coin** was made in Lydia, Turkey, around 670 B.C. It was stamped with the symbol of King Gyges, which was a lion.

Wind Up a Whirligig

A whirligig is a toy that makes a buzzing noise when you pull it. Kids have been making whirligigs for more than 200 years. You can make a whirligig by recycling things found around your house.

You will need:
lid of a yogurt container
stickers and markers
scissors
string
masking tape
pushpin

Decorate both sides of the lid any way you like. **Cut** the string 2 arm-lengths long (about 40 inches). **Put** a piece of tape on both sides of the lid — this will make it stronger. **Use** the pushpin to poke 2 holes near the center of the lid about ¼ inch apart.

Thread the string through the holes and **tie** the ends to make a loop. The loop should be as **long** as your shoulders are wide.

Everyday tips for recycling:
Use both sides of a piece of paper.
Take a cloth bag with you when you go shopping.
Have a yard sale.
Turn old clothes into rags for messy projects or cleaning.
Use cloth towels instead of paper towels.

Hold one end of the loop with each hand so that the lid is hanging between your hands. **Swing** the lid around many times in one direction to wind up your whirligig. Once the string is **wound** up, quickly pull both ends of the string. **Move** your hands together and apart as the lid spins around. The lid will whirl for a long time. (It may take a while to get the hang of this.)

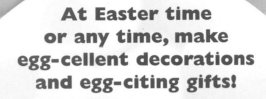

Glamorous Glitter Eggs

At Easter time or any time, make egg-cellent decorations and egg-citing gifts!

You will need:

several eggs • straight pin (as used in sewing) • glue paintbrush • glitter • waxed paper

Hold an egg over a bowl. **Make** a hole in the narrow end of the egg by pushing and twisting with the pin. Then **flip** the egg over and make a similar hole in the wide end of the egg. **Enlarge** this hole just a bit by chipping away at the shell. **Break** the yolk inside the egg by sticking it with the pin. Next, over a bowl, **blow** into the hole at the narrow end of the egg until you have blown all the insides out of the wide end.

Brush your egg with glue. Then gently **set** it in a bowl of glitter. **Roll** your egg around in the glitter until it is completely covered. **Set** it on a piece of waxed paper to dry for about an hour. You might also **experiment** by mixing several colors of glitter and covering an egg. Or you could **brush** glue on the top half of an egg, **roll** it in one color of glitter, and **repeat** the process with a different color of glitter on the bottom half.

P.S. Don't throw out the insides of the egg — save them in the fridge to make one of the yummy recipes in the **Bake It!** section, such as Supersoft Pretzels or Lasagna Roll-Ups.

Zfact: In the Ukraine, egg decorating, or *pysanky,* is a folk art passed down from generation to generation. To decorate eggs, Ukrainians use candle wax, colored dyes, and a small writing instrument called a *kistka.* Designs can take hours to create and include many, many layers of wax and dyes. Dye colors are chosen for symbolic reasons: red for love, pink for success, blue for health, and yellow for spirituality. The eggs are given as gifts at Easter, but are enjoyed all year long.

Delightful Decoupage Jar

Sent in by Killian C. of Portland, Oregon.

To decoupage the jar, you will need:

- colored tissue paper
- glue
- paper cup
- paintbrush
- glass jar with a lid

Rip tissue paper into small pieces. **Squirt** some glue into a cup and add a little water. **Stir** with a paintbrush. Brush the mixture onto the jar. Then **press** the tissue paper pieces onto the jar. You can **overlap** them to create different colors. **Cover** the entire jar. When you're finished, **brush** a coat of the glue mixture over the whole jar — this will **seal** it. Let your jar dry for a couple of hours. Be sure not to cover the edges of the lid with paper or you won't be able to open your jar!

P.S. For the perfect homemade gift, fill your jar with Cozy Cocoa Mix and add a gift card with cooking instructions.

Cozy Cocoa Mix

You will need:

- 1/4 cup powdered cocoa (unsweetened)
- 1/4 cup powdered sugar
- 1 cup powdered milk
- hot water
- marshmallows (optional)

Ask an adult to help you heat the water. Mix all ingredients together. **Place** 3 tablespoons of cocoa mix in mug. **Pour** in 8 ounces of hot water and stir. Add marshmallows, if you want! That's it!

Sent in by the Zeller family of La Porte, Indiana

Dream Catcher

Sent in by Becky R. of Jackson, New Jersey.

Native American tradition says that if you hang a Dream Catcher above your bed, the Dream Catcher will catch good dreams and let the bad ones go through the holes. Here's how to make your very own.

You will need:
paper plate
single-hole puncher
yarn
beads, feathers, and markers

Make the Frame
Cut out the center of the paper plate so that you have about 2 inches of the rim left over. **Punch** holes around the rim of the plate. Make the holes about an inch apart.

Weave a Web
Cut a piece of yarn that is about 2 arm-lengths long. Tie one end of the yarn to one of the holes. Start **weaving** the yarn across the plate from one hole to the next. Make it **overlap** a few times so it looks like a web. You can **add** a few beads to your Dream Catcher by slipping them onto the yarn as you weave. When you're done, tie a knot at the end of the yarn.

Add Some Style
Punch 3 more holes at the bottom of your Dream Catcher. Tie about 5 inches of yarn to each of the holes. **Thread** beads onto each piece of yarn and tie a feather to the end. Use markers to **decorate** the paper plate. **Punch** a hole at the top of the Dream Catcher. Put a piece of yarn through the hole and tie it to make a small **loop.** Hang your Dream Catcher over your bed to ward off nightmares. **Sweet Dreams!**

Zoops

"My most embarrassing moment was when my cousin pushed me off the diving board and my pants fell off."
-Alex H. of Hialeah, Florida

Bubble Stationery

Sent in by Morgan P. of Bethesda, Maryland.

Next time you write a letter to someone, jazz it up with Bubble Stationery.

You will need:
dishwashing liquid
food coloring
paper cups
straws
blank paper
newspaper

Mix dishwashing liquid and a few drops of food coloring in a paper cup. **Dip** a straw in the cup, then blow bubbles through the straw onto a piece of paper. (Make sure you blow out of the straw. Do not suck in—dishwashing liquid tastes terrible!) **Repeat** with another color. Experiment and see what different kinds of designs and color combinations you can make. **Leave** your stationery on some newspaper to dry.

P.S. This paper is great for thank-you notes!

Here's a **ZOOMzinger** from Rebecca P. of Concord, Massachusetts:

What stays in the corner but goes all around the world?

Answer: A stamp.

Carefully take **apart** the envelope so that it lies flat. This will be your pattern. **Tear** a page from a magazine or calendar with a colorful picture or design on it. **Place** the envelope pattern on top of this page and trace around it with a marker. **Cut** it out. **Fold** the flaps over and glue the side flaps to the bottom flap. Be careful not to get glue on the inside of your envelope. **Press** down on the glued areas and then let the envelope dry for a while. To **use** the envelope, put your letter in, **fold** the top over it, and glue, tape, or sticker the envelope shut. Print your address in a dark marker or put a label on it so the letter carrier can read it. **Head for the mailbox!**

You'll need an envelope to mail your bubble letter. Why not make one yourself?

You will need:
envelope to use as a pattern
old calendars or magazines
marker
scissors
glue stick

Make Your Own Envelope

Here's a **ZOOMzinger** from Deanna and Alena R. of Akron, Ohio:

What word starts with an "E," and has only one letter in it?

Answer: Envelope.

Create Your Own Kaleidoscope

Sent in by Claudia M. of Buena Park, California.

You will need:

- masking tape
- 3 small rectangular mirrors (You can find these at a drugstore.)
- clear, sticky lamination paper (You can find this at a hardware or housewares store. It's also called shelf liner.)
- clear plastic wrap
- scissors
- glitter, paper shapes, small beads, confetti
- clear tape
- black construction paper
- white crayon

Use masking tape to tape the 3 mirrors together the long way. The reflecting sides should **face** in so that they form a tent shape.

Using the end of your tent shape as a pattern, **trace** 2 triangles on the lamination paper and 1 on the plastic wrap.

Cut out the triangles. **Peel** off the backing from 1 of the laminated triangles and turn it sticky-side up. **Sprinkle** glitter and small bits of colored paper on it. Then **make** a sandwich by peeling the other laminated triangle and placing it sticky-side down on top. **Arrange** beads and more confetti on top of your glitter sandwich. **Use** clear tape to fasten the plastic-wrap triangle on top. Using clear tape again, **tape** the entire packet to the end of the mirror tent.

Lay the kaleidoscope on its side on a piece of black construction paper. **Continue** tracing as you carefully roll it over 2 times. **Cut** out the paper — it should be just the right size to cover the sides of your kaleidoscope. Tape it tightly around the outside of the mirrors.

Hold your kaleidoscope up to the light and take a look. **Turn** it around slowly. **Share** your kaleidoscope and dazzle your friends and family.

Zfact:

Scottish scientist Sir David Brewster **invented** the kaleidoscope in 1816. He made this discovery while conducting experiments with light.

Sent in by Nathan S. of Onawa, Iowa.

Wonderful Wind Chimes

Wind chimes make great gifts and are a super way to recycle. Even better, they can help scare away birds and other animals that might otherwise munch on your garden.

You will need:
- objects to hang as chimes: old silverware, empty soda cans, old CDs, old keys, or anything else that might make a nice noise
- acrylic paint
- paintbrush
- hanger
- string

Paint items and hanger any way you like. When items have dried, **tie** a piece of string onto each one. Strings should vary in length. **Tie** the strings to the hanger, attaching the heaviest items toward the middle to keep things balanced. **Hold** your wind chimes up in the wind and see if you like the sound they make. Make changes if necessary. **Enjoy!**

oops

"My most embarrassing moment was when my sister told the boy I liked that I liked him."
—Martina G. of San Diego, California

Save-It-All Scrapbook

Sent in by Jill G. of South Orange, New Jersey.

Keep your favorite memories in this Save-It-All Scrapbook you can make yourself.

FRONT AND BACK COVER

Measure and cut 2 pieces of cardboard so that they are a bit larger than your construction paper. They should measure about 10 inches by 13 inches. These pieces will be the front and back covers of your book. **Punch** 3 holes in the left side of both covers. **Lay** the fabric pieces flat and place a piece of cardboard on top of each. Trace around the cardboard, leaving a 2-inch border around it. **Cut** out the fabric. **Lay** 1 cardboard piece on top of 1 piece of fabric. **Spread** a little glue around the edges of the cardboard that are facing up. Then fold the fabric over so that it covers the entire front of the cardboard. **Repeat** this with the other cover. **Glue** a piece of construction paper on both pieces of cardboard so that it overlaps the fabric edges. This makes it look finished on the inside and helps to keep the fabric in place. **Feel** along the edge of the covers for the punched holes. **Cut** slits in the fabric over the holes with scissors.

You will need:
- ruler
- scissors
- cardboard (Pieces of a cardboard box work well.)
- fabric
- glue
- construction paper
- envelopes with metal clasps on the back
- hole puncher and reinforcements
- ribbon

THE INSIDE

Use construction paper for the pages on which you want to glue things. If you want to save things like letters and report cards but don't want to glue them, put them in envelopes. **Punch** 3 holes in the left sides of the pieces of paper and/or envelopes. **Put** them in order between the covers. **Thread** a piece of ribbon through each of the 3 holes and tie them to hold your book together.

P.S. You might want to think of a theme for your scrapbook, like "School Days" with sections for each grade. Special trips or a special friendship also make fun themes.

You could even ubbify or dubbify part of your scrapbook!

Versatile Vegetable Prints

Sent in by Stephanie R. of Ayer, Massachusetts.

You will need:

- knife
- vegetables, such as potatoes, onions, peppers, or string beans
- paper towels
- several small disposable dishes
- ink, tempera paint, or food coloring
- paper

Eating vegetables may be good for your health, but painting with vegetables is just plain fun!

ASK an adult to help you cut some vegetables in half. If you choose a potato, ask an adult to help you **carve** a design into the flat side of the potato — **cut** away the parts you don't want to print. You could also use a **melon baller** to carve out the middle of a potato.

Make your own ink pads by folding 1 or 2 paper towels and placing them in a dish. **Add** ink, tempera paint, or food coloring to the towels. Use a different dish for each color. **Pick** up your veggies and start printing. You **might** want to use your prints to decorate cards, make your own wrapping paper, or just create some stunning artwork.

P.S. If you have fabric paint, print some vegetables on a plain T-shirt or some dish towels.

"See a star when you print with an apple stamp. Just cut the apple in half horizontally and print."
—Armide S. of Essex, Massachusetts

Fanneed Doolee

likes **cabbage** but doesn't like **vegetables.** Why do you think that is?

Sent in by Madison E. of Denver, Colorado.

Push-Pull Card

Is there a special occasion coming up? Want to wow a friend? Make a Push-Pull Card!

You will need:

- piece of paper
- thin cardboard
- scissors
- hole puncher
- brass paper fastener
- markers
- tape or glue

If you had fun making this card and want to try your hand at pop-ups, check out any of these books:

Pop-O-Mania by Barbara Valenta; Dial Books for Young Readers.

How to Make Pop-Ups by Joan Irvine, illustrated by Barbara Reid; Morrow Junior Books.

How to Make Holiday Pop-Ups by Joan Irvine, illustrated by Lisa Hendry; Morrow Junior Books.

1 **Fold** a piece of paper in half and then in half again. This will be your card. **Cut** shapes like those below out of your thin cardboard.

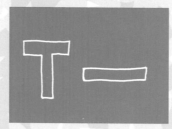

2 **Punch** a hole in the center of the T-shaped piece. **Punch** 2 holes in the straight piece and use the scissors to connect them, making a little slot.

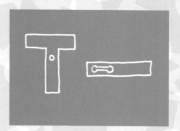

3 Then **slide** the T-shaped piece into the slot of the straight piece — see below. This will be your **handle:**

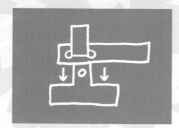

4 **Punch** a hole in the center of the front of the card. (The hole puncher won't reach that far, so it's best just to poke a hole with the brass fastener.) Then **cut** a slot above the hole, like this:

5 **Slide** the handle under the piece of paper at the front of the card, making sure the holes line up. Slide the brass fastener through the front of the card and **fasten.** Make sure the end of the T-shape is sticking through the slot you just cut in the card. This is where your shape will move back and forth. Then **cut** a shape out of cardboard and decorate it. Tape the shape onto the cardboard tab (the end of the T-shape). **Push and pull** gently to make your shape move.

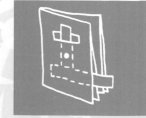

SNOW GLOBE

Sent in by Rachel S. of Rice Lake, Wisconsin.

It can snow any time of the year when you have a Snow Globe. So get shaking!

Use duct tape to attach a small plastic toy or two to the inside of the lid. Then **fill** the jar with water. **Pour** some glitter in the water. **Take** the lid with the toys attached to it and screw it tightly onto the jar. **Turn** the jar upside down. **Watch** it start snowing! Lastly, paint a scene on the outside of the jar and let it **dry** overnight. There you have it — your own snowy little world inside a jar.

You will need:
- duct tape
- small plastic toys
- small jar with a lid
- glitter
- paint
- paintbrush

Zoinks!

What does it take to get a job making ZOOM?
We asked the people who make ZOOM what jobs they used to have. Here are some of their replies: singer in a rock band, bank teller, whale tagger, dairy farm worker, bakery cashier, radio disc jockey, psychiatric hospital worker, skateboard maker, wardrobe supervisor for the Boston Ballet, assembly line worker in a food factory, lifeguard, model, waitress, poet, and lighting technician on movies such as *True Lies, The Firm,* and *Glory*.

Breezy Ballo

This car doesn't need gas. It runs on balloon power! Show a friend how to build a balloon car and then see whose car travels farther.

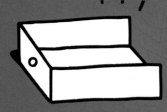

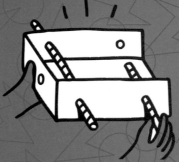

Car body

Cut off the top of the carton. Then cut the carton in half the long way. **Poke** a hole in the center of the carton's bottom with a pair of scissors. The neck of the balloon will go through this hole. The open side of the carton should face up.

Wheels and axles

Make 2 holes for the straw axles in each side of the carton. Put one near the front of the carton, and the other near the back. The holes should be close enough to the carton floor to allow the spools to touch the ground. Insert the straws. (A wide carton may require 2 straws taped together for each axle.) **Slide** spools onto the axles. To keep spools from rolling off and touching the body of the car, **push** straight pins through the straws on the outside and inside of each spool. Make sure the spools can still spin freely.

Fuel tank

Push the open end of the balloon through the hole in the bottom of the carton. The balloon should be lying inside the carton. The balloon will hold the air that powers your car. **Decorate** your car if you like.

Ask an adult to help you build this Breezy Balloon Car.

The force of the escaping air causes the balloon to move in the direction opposite the rushing air.

n Car

You will need:

- any size milk or juice carton (rinsed and dried)
- scissors
- 2 or 4 plastic drinking straws
- masking tape
- 4 empty wooden or plastic thread spools
- 8 straight pins
- balloon (any size)
- ruler

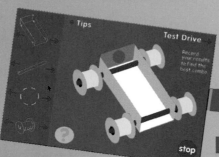

Start your engine!

Blow up the balloon and hold the end tightly. **Place** the car on the floor at a starting line marked with tape and release the balloon. **Measure** the distance your car travels. **Compare** distance with a friend's car or race yours again to see if it goes any farther. If you like, experiment by making adjustments on your car. What would happen if the carton were shaped differently? What if the balloon exhaust hole were smaller or larger?

If you had fun making the balloon car and want to do some more experimenting with just the click of a mouse, download the Virtual Balloon Car from the ZOOM Web site at **pbskids.org/zoom** You can click to adjust various features of the virtual car and then race it again and again!

"I tried three balloons on my car. I think the air going in different directions made it go slower instead of faster."
— Cela from Rochester, New York

"My Virtual Balloon Car went twelve meters!"
— E-mail from Dylan S.

With just a rubber band and some Styrofoam, you can make a boat that will sail all on its own.

You will need:

Styrofoam tray • scissors • rubber band • bathtub or wading pool filled with water

Cut the Styrofoam tray into a boat shape. Then **cut** a large square out of the back end of the boat. Later your paddle wheel will be attached here.

Cut out 2 rectangles from the leftover Styrofoam. Then **cut** a small piece out of the middle of each rectangle.

Fit the rectangles together. This is the paddle wheel that will power your boat.

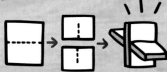

Stretch the rubber band across the back end of the boat and over the rectangular gap. Next, **take** your paddle wheel and **slip** it between the sides of the rubber band.

Z fact:

Paddle-wheel boats, also called steamboats, were used in the nineteenth and early twentieth centuries to carry passengers and goods over lakes and large rivers. They were powered by steam engines. Steamboat travel was especially popular on the Mississippi and Missouri Rivers.

Peppy Paddle-Wheel Boat

Sent in by Patrick C. of the Greenup County CES 4-H in Flatwoods, Kentucky.

Turn the paddle several times to wind up your boat. **Set** it in the water and let 'er rip! **Show** a friend how to make a paddle-wheel boat and have a race. Or see how far or fast you can get your paddle-wheel boat to travel.

Compass in a Dish

Sent in by Sarah N.
of Kenbridge, Virginia.

Think a needle is only good for sewing? Think again. With just a few steps you can turn a sewing needle into a reliable compass.

You will need:
- small piece of Styrofoam
- bowl of water
- magnet
- sewing needle
- masking tape

Float the Styrofoam in the bowl of water. Pick up the magnet in one hand and the needle in the other. **Stroke** the needle along one end of the magnet 20 times or more in the same direction. (Do not rub both up and down the magnet!) When you're finished, **place** the needle on top of the Styrofoam. Use a small piece of masking tape to mark the edge of the bowl where the needle is pointing. **Turn** the bowl or the Styrofoam and watch what happens to the needle. It will always turn to point in the same directic **just like a compass.**

Do you want to do another **experiment** with your magnet? Make another needle magnet. Point it close to your first **needle magnet** as it floats. Watch and see if the magnets move toward each other **(attract)** or move away from each other **(repel).** Every magnet has a south pole and a north pole. When you put like poles of 2 magnets together, they repel; opposite poles attract each other.

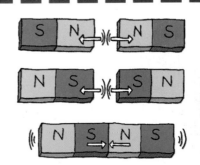

Sent in by Rebecca B. and Anna V. of Longview, Texas.

Biodome

You will need:

- three 2-liter soda bottles
- marker
- 2 bottle caps
- thumbtack
- scissors
- thick cotton string
- tape
- potting soil
- seeds (like dried beans)

When you grow plants in a biodome, you never need to water them.

Take the labels off of the soda bottles and **mark** them A, B, and C. Cut them as shown in the illustrations below:

Attach the cap to Bottle B. **Invert** Bottle B into Bottle C. The bottle cap should touch the top of the water. **Tape** the bottles together.

Add a few handfuls of dirt to Bottle B. Make sure that the string runs up into the middle of the soil and is not stuck along the side of the bottle.

Poke a ¾-inch-deep hole in the soil and drop in some seeds. **Cover** the seeds with soil and add a little water until the soil is moist.

Pour water into Bottle C so that it's half full. **Poke** a hole in one bottle cap and **enlarge** it with scissors so you can push the string through. **Soak** the string in water and run it through the hole in the cap. The string will draw water into the soil.

26

A (lid)

A

B

C

Put Bottle A on top of Bottle B and tape them together. **Tape** the top that you cut off Bottle A to the rest of the bottle structure. Screw on the cap.

Everything your plants need to live—soil, air, and water—is inside the biodome. Now all your biodome **needs** is a sunny spot so it can use sunlight to make its own food.

P.S. Plant fast-growing seeds, like radishes, in your biodome and in a flowerpot. Plant them at the same time and keep them in the same place. Watch to see which plants grow faster. Why do you think this is?

"I only used two pop bottles and it worked just as well I used cress and radish seeds. They grew about four inches tall. Every day the water evaporates, forms a slight fog, and then 'rains.' It's really cool."
— E-mail from Katie P. of Columbia Station, Ohio

"I planted bean seeds in my biodome and they sprouted in three days! By day five, I had to take the biodome cover off because they grew really tall!"
— E-mail from Gina U. of Walpole, Massachusetts

Sent in by Andie B. of Princeton, New Jersey.

A Poem

Tree

I planted a seed down below,

and now I want to help it grow.

It grows from bottom
to middle to top,

and now I don't want to
let it stop.

It's growing and growing
so now it's real big,

but now it's not
like it was before…

It's the size of a
DINOSAUR!!!!!!!!!!!!!!!!!

27

POtatO BattEry

Ask an adult to help you build this Potato Battery.

You will need:

- baking potato
- about 2 feet of 18-gauge copper wire cut into 4 equal pieces
- wire cutters
- 2 galvanized nails
- 2 pennies
- small digital clock or watch

A potato is delicious for dinner— but it can also make a great battery!

Cut the potato in half horizontally and place the cut ends down on a plate. **Wrap** a piece of wire a few times around a galvanized nail. **Wrap** another piece of wire a few times around a penny. Then **stick** the nail and penny into the same potato half, but make sure that they aren't touching.

Wrap a piece of wire around the second penny, but not the second nail. **Stick** the penny and nail into the other half of the potato as before. Then **connect** the wire from the penny in the first half of the potato to the nail in the other half of the potato. **Remove** the battery from the clock or watch. **Connect** the unattached wires from the penny and the nail to the battery contacts on the clock or watch. Your potato battery should turn it on. If it doesn't, try reconnecting the wires in the reverse direction. Electricity flows in one direction only and you may have hooked it up the wrong way.

P.S. Try making a battery in this same fashion with a small flashlight bulb and a lemon or orange.

Why can you make a battery out of a potato? **Chemicals** in the potato react with the copper penny and send **electricity** to the steel nail and on to the other penny and finally into the clock and out—back to the first penny. If any of the wires in this pattern, or circuit, are removed, the battery won't work.

Meet Jesse
Glider Pilot

Q: How old are you and where do you live?
Jesse: I'm twelve years old, and I live in Lincoln, Rhode Island.

Q: What's a glider?
Jesse: A glider is basically an airplane that you throw. When you throw it, a lot of air catches underneath it and picks it up. Gliders can be pretty simple and still work.

Q: What kinds of materials do you use to build your gliders?
Jesse: I use all kinds of different things, like toothpicks, newspaper, plastic, duct tape, aluminum foil, index cards, plastic milk jugs, and soda bottles. I made one glider out of furniture wire, a matchbox, electrical tape, and index cards.

Q: What do you like best about making gliders?
Jesse: When you make gliders, you start to learn a lot about what makes a plane fly. A lot of times a glider won't work and will just crash. Then you just go back and work on it some more. It's fun to try making different models, like a dart plane or a biplane. If you put wings on it and you can throw it, you can usually make it fly.

z fact:
Gliders soar on rising currents of warm air. A glider big enough to carry a person can dive as fast as 200 mph and cruise at about 100 mph. However, a Boeing 747 can fly 580 mph with more than 400 passengers and their luggage, and a Concorde jet can fly 1,336 mph, faster than the speed of sound.

Sent in by David E. of South Bend, Indiana.

You will need:
- piece of standard 8½" × 11" paper
- scissors
- paper clip

A Fast-Flying Paper Airplane

The D-400

Follow these simple instructions and launch a paper airplane of your own.

Fold your piece of paper in half the long way, then **open** it back up. **Fold** the top corners of the paper in toward the middle so you have 2 triangles at the top.

Fold the triangles in half, in toward the middle.

Fold each triangle in again.

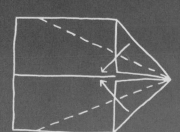

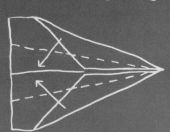

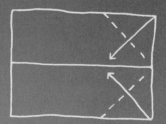

Flying

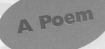
A Poem

Gliding high above their heads,
I can feel the wind beating on my face,
It has endless rhythms,
Whistling in my ears,
I feel free to be soaring through the cool,
Dark air.
I see a star that twinkles and turns before
My eyes.
My arms are now up and down,
Up and down with tremendous strength,
My legs fly loosely out behind me.
I twist and turn making spirals in the night air.

Sent in by Emily L. of
Acton, Massachusetts.

Fold the plane in half, the opposite way.

Flip it over and **open** up the wings. **Cut** a flap on the end of each wing. **Bend** one flap so it faces up, and **bend** the other flap so it faces down.

Clip a paper clip to the bottom of the plane.

Throw the plane hard but smoothly and watch it **spin** and swerve through the air.

Stunt Flyer

Ray showed us how to make this cool trick plane. All you need is a standard 8½" x 11" piece of paper.

1

Take your piece of paper and **fold** the left corner down to make a triangle, leaving some space at the bottom.

2

Fold the top part of the triangle over, making a smaller triangle.

3

Fold down the tip of the triangle until it touches the bottom edge of the triangle.

4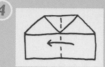

Fold the whole thing in half, so that the flaps are on the inside.

5

Here's the tricky part: **Fold** back one wing, leaving ½ inch for the body of the plane. Then **fold** back the other wing so you have a V in the middle.

6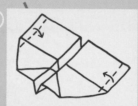

Finally, **fold** a small flap to stand upright on the end of each wing. Now you're ready for **takeoff!**

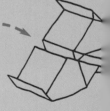

If you feel like more folding, check out these books or Web sites:

Fold-and-Fly Paper Airplanes by Franco Pavarin and Luciano Spaggian; Sterling Publishing Co. Inc.

Planes and Other Flying Things by Florence Temko; The Milbrook Press.

Kids' Paper Airplane Book by Ken Blackburn and Jeff Lammers; Workman Publishing Co.

Super Paper Airplanes: Biplanes to Space Planes by Norman Schmidt; Sterling Publishing Co. Inc.

Ken Blackburn's Web site
http://www.geocities.com/CapeCanaveral/1817

Paper Airplane Hangar
http://www.tycs.demon.co.uk/planes

Name two things you would pack on a trip to Mars and explain why.

"I would pack my PlayStation so I wouldn't be bored and a phone to call my mom so she wouldn't be lonely."
— Keith J. of East Rochester, New York

"Soccer ball and pillow because I could play and sleep."
— Alison M. of Martinez, Georgia

"I would bring my blanket and my best friend, Rachel, because I like my friend and I like my blanket."
— Lara T. of Martinez, Georgia

"Food and a very long book. Food because you need to eat and a book because I love to read."
— Sanford W. of Columbia, Maryland

Zoinks!

What would you take with you on a long rocket trip?

Here's what some of the folks who make ZOOM would take into outer space: **popcorn,** Scrabble and Tang, **the New York Public Library,** the top 100 movies, **crossword puzzles,** dance shoes, **quilting fabric,** ice cream, **art supplies,** change of address forms for the post office, **sushi,** and Bob Dylan CDs.

How about you?

Zfact:

On December 2, 1996, NASA launched the **Mars Pathfinder.** About 7 months later, on July 4, 1997, it landed on Mars. It carried a 6-wheeled rover named **Sojourner.** **Sojourner** explored the planet's surface and sent images and information back to Earth for scientists to study. See photos of Mars on the Web at **http://mars.jpl.nasa.gov.**

Whizzing Waterwheel

A waterwheel uses water to create power to move things. Most electric companies use water power, which is also called hydroelectric power. They build dams to harness the water power created by rivers. Make this whizzing waterwheel and see what you can get it to lift.

You will need:

- pint-sized milk carton
- scissors
- duct tape
- pencil (new or almost new)
- a load to lift with your waterwheel, like a bag of marbles
- string
- 2 quart-sized milk cartons
- ruler
- watering can and a place where you can pour water (such as outdoors or in a bathtub)

The wheel

Cut a door into each side of the small carton. Make sure all the doors open in the same direction. **Open** the doors.

Fold the top of the carton down so it doesn't stick up anymore. **Tape** it down. Use scissors to **poke** a pencil-width hole in the top and bottom of your carton. **Slide** the pencil through the holes.

e load

...nd a bag of marbles or ...mething else for your ...terwheel to lift. This is called ...e load. **Tie** the load to the ...nd of a 2-foot-long piece of ...tring. **Tie** and **tape** the ...tring to the pencil.

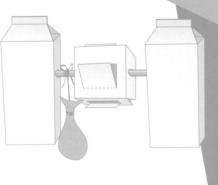

The stand

The larger cartons will hold up your wheel. **Poke** a pencil-width hole in 1 side of each carton, 6 inches up from the bottom. **Put** the pencil ends into these 2 holes.

The action

Fill the larger cartons with water or sand to weigh them down, or have someone hold them. **Bring** your waterwheel outside or to the bathtub. **Pour** water over the wheel and watch your waterwheel work. How many marbles can it **lift?** Try lifting other loads and see what happens.

"When I did this I got it to lift a pair of shoes!"
— E-mail from Hunter W. of Birmingham, Alabama

"We put it in the bathtub. We hit it with the shower hose, turned on to 'really powerful,' and the wheel went ZOOMING around very fast!"
— E-mail from Charlie B. of Madison, Wisconsin

"It worked and it carried 67 pennies."
— E-mail from Mathew M. of New York, New York

Drinking Fountain
a poem

Sent in by Tiffany W. of Greensboro, North Carolina.

When I climb up to
get a drink it doesn't
work the way you think
I turn it, up the water
goes and hits me right
upon the nose and I turn it
down to make it small
and don't get any
drink at all.

Fannee Doolee

likes **swimming,** but doesn't like **water.** Why do you think that is?

— Sent in by Madison E. of Denver, Colorado.

35

The Amazing Lung-Capacity Machine

Sent in by Rebecca G. of Parsippany, New Jersey.

Have you ever wondered how much air you can hold in your lungs? Build this simple Lung-Capacity Machine and find out.

You will need:

- washbasin
- water
- gallon-sized milk jug
- measuring cup
- rubber tube
- paper towel
- rubbing alcohol

The setup

Fill the washbasin with water until it is about an inch deep. Fill the jug with 16 cups of water. **Insert** a rubber tube into the opening of the jug. Holding the tube in the mouth of the jug, quickly **turn** the jug upside down to place the opening underwater in the washbasin.

The action

Take a deep breath and blow into the other end of the tube until your breath runs out. Then **flip** the jug back upright and measure the water left in the jug using the measuring cup. **Subtract** the amount of water left in the jug from the original 16 cups. The answer reveals how many cups of air you have in your lungs. Use the paper towel and alcohol to **wipe** the tube clean for the next person.

P.S. See if you can guess which of your friends or family members has more air in their lungs. Does height make a difference? How about physical fitness?

Zfacts:

In the lungs, the blood exchanges waste for oxyg[en]. When you breathe in, your lu[ngs] take in oxygen, which the bl[ood] whisks away to nourish the re[st of] the body. Meanwhile, the bloo[d] carried waste, like carbon dio[xide] to the lungs so you can breat[he] out and rid your body of i[t].

Yogis (yoga teachers) say that the best breathing ratio is **1 to 2**. In other words, your breath out should be twice as long as your breath in. Deep breathing helps to develop the muscles around the lungs. It is also calming and relaxing. Give it a try!

Quick Can Car

Sent in by Sarah G. of St. Louis, Missouri

[bu]ild a car and see how far and how fast you can get it [to] go. Challenge a friend to a race. Here's how to make one: [b]upubon yubour mubark, gubet subet, gubo!

[Ask] an adult to help you use a can opener to remove the bottom of [an e]mpty coffee can. The edges can be sharp.

[Pu]nch a hole in the center of both lids with a pair of [scis]sors. The hole needs to be large enough to allow the rubber [ban]d to twist inside the hole. **Slip** a rubber band through [on]e of the holes and hook it around a paper clip on the outside [of] the lid. **Tape** the paper clip to the lid and put the lid [ba]ck on the coffee can.

[Sl]ip the other end of the rubber band through the can [an]d out the other side through the hole in the other lid. [Th]en **slip** the rubber band through a bead on the outside [o]f the lid. **Attach** that lid to the can. **Slip** a pencil [t]hrough the end of the rubber band next to the bead. **[P]ut** a little liquid soap around the edges of that end of the [c]an to cut down on rubbing, so the pencil will turn more [s]moothly. **Wind up** the pencil several [t]imes — until it comes back to [y]ou freely. Then **put** the Can Car on the table or floor. Let go and your car will take off!

You will need:

- coffee can and
  2 coffee can lids
- can opener
- scissors
- rubber band
- paper clip
- masking tape
- bead
- pencil
- liquid soap

Salt Pendulum

"My friend, my sister, and I made a salt pendulum. We put clear glue all over the black paper so the salt would stick. We used colored sand mixed with salt instead. It was cool."
—E-mail from Loretta B. of Eastport, Maine

A pendulum swings back and forth freely from a fixed point. Think of the pendulum that keeps time inside a grandfather clock. This Salt Pendulum below draws pictures.

You will need:

- construction paper
- tape
- string
- doorway (for setting up)
- salt
- broom (for cleaning up)
  optional: newspaper
  (to cover the area for easier cleanup)

Z facts:

Salt usually makes up 3% of ocean water, but the Great Salt Lake is made up of a whopping 12% salt. This very salty water is much denser than freshwater, which makes it really easy for swimmers to float.

Cakes of salt were used as money in ancient Ethiopia and Tibet.

1

The cone

Roll a piece of construction paper to form a cone. **Tape** the sides of the cone closed, but leave a small hole at the tip. **Cut** 3 pieces of string to the same length. Tape one end of each string to the inside of the open end of the cone. **Tie** the loose ends of the 3 strings together.

The setup 2

Cut a 4th piece of string and tape it to an open door frame so that it **forms** a hanging arc. Tie another string to the point where the 3 strings taped to the cone are joined. Then tie this string to the middle of the hanging arc. Make sure the cone does not **touch** the floor.

The action 3

Put black construction paper on the floor under the cone. **Pinch** the hole in the tip of the cone closed while you fill it with salt. Let go of the hole and give the pendulum a gentle **push.** Watch and see what kind of design it makes.

P.S. Does it make a regular pattern? Why do you think that is? Can you make changes to your pendulum so it creates different patterns?

Sites to Surf for More Crafts and Experiments

If you want to **discover** more crafts and experiments on your own, **check out** these super Web sites. If you don't have Internet access at home, ask at your school or local library.

Exploratorium
http://netra.exploratorium.edu
Web site of the Exploratorium, a fantastic museum of science, art, and human perception located in San Francisco. Check out the Digital Library or visit the Learning Studio.

Homearts Network Rainy Day Projects
http://homearts.com/depts/family/00rain51.htm
Targeted to parents, includes directions for making a variety of craft and science projects.

BOAST
http://boast.ccsm.uiuc.edu
Includes instructions for building a number of physics-related projects.

Chem4Kids
http://www.chem4kids.com
Explore the basics of chemistry.

How Things Work
http://howthingswork.virginia.edu
Have your physics questions answered by a university professor.

The Knowledge Adventure Encyclopedia
http://letsfindout.com
Gives you access to all kinds of cool information on a variety of topics.

MAD Scientist Network
http://www.madsci.org
Features the MadSci Library for finding science resources on the Web, as well as "Ask-A-Scientist."

Zoinks!

Can you touch your nose with your tongue?

We asked the people who make ZOOM the same question. 14% said they could. Hmmm...

Supersoft Pretzels

Sent in by Dana P. of Poulsbo, Washington.

You will need:

- 1 packet of yeast
- 1½ cups slightly warm water
- 1 tablespoon sugar
- 1 tablespoon salt
  (Kosher salt is best.)
- 4 cups flour
- 1 egg

Ask an adult for help with the oven.

Preheat the oven to 425 degrees. **Mix** the yeast, water, sugar, and salt together. Yeast smells weird, but don't worry—the pretzels will taste good. **Add** the flour. **Knead** the dough with your hands on a floured surface until it's smooth.

Tear off pieces and make them into shapes, like your initials, or **twist** them around in the traditional pretzel shape. Be sure **not** to make the pieces too thick or they'll taste doughy. And if they're too thin they'll break. About a 1-inch thickness is good.

Put the pretzels on a cookie sheet. Slightly beat the egg and **brush** it onto the pretzels. (You can also use the back of a spoon to do this.) **Sprinkle** them with salt—kosher salt is great for this because the crystals are bigger than regular salt crystals.

Bake the pretzels for 12–15 minutes or until they're golden brown. When they're done, carefully remove them from the oven and let them **cool** before munching.

zfacts

The **first pretzel bakery was founded in 1861** in Lititz, Pennsylvania, by Julius Sturgis.

The pretzel's shape is based on an ancient prayer position in which arms were folded across the chest and hands placed on shoulders. Originally, pretzels were eaten during Lent.

These pretzels taste good—soft on the top and crunchy on the bottom.

The Ultimate ZOOMparty Menu

Invite a few friends over and party down with these fun-to-fix-and-more-fun-to-eat party foods!

Pigs in a Blanket

Sent in by Nicholas R. of West Jordan, Utah.

You will need:
- hot dogs
- slices of cheese
- package of crescent roll dough

Ask an adult to help you with the oven and with cutting the hot dogs.

Preheat the oven to 375 degrees. Make a **slit** down the long side of a hot dog, being careful not to slice all the way through. **Tuck** a piece of cheese in the slit. Separate the crescent roll dough. Put the hot dog on a piece of dough and **roll** it up. Place the pig in a blanket on an ungreased cookie sheet. Repeat with as many hot dogs as desired. **Bake** for 12–15 minutes or until dough is golden brown.

Onion Dip

Sent in by Tracy J.

A party just wouldn't be a party without chips and dip!

You will need:
- chips or raw veggies
- $\frac{1}{2}$ cup mayonnaise
- $\frac{1}{2}$ cup cream cheese
- 1 onion, chopped
- 1 teaspoon dry onion soup mix

Arrange chips or vegetables on a large plate or in a shallow bowl. **Mix** mayonnaise, cream cheese, onion, and soup mix in a smaller bowl and place it in the center of the chips or veggies for dipping.

Ginger Ale–Raspberry Punch

You will need:

- ginger ale
- raspberry sherbet

Pour ginger ale into a punch bowl. **Add** sherbet and serve.

You can make funky ice cubes to keep your punch cold by freezing fruit juice or by filling an ice tray with water and adding a berry to each cube before freezing.

Here's a joke by Akash P. of Fremont, California:

What do you call a cold hot dog?

Answer: A chill dog!

Fannee Doolee

likes **cherries** but doesn't like **fruit.** Why do you think that is?

Sent in by Stephanie H. of Apopka, Florida.

Cranberry-Lemon Punch

Sent in by Callie O. of Edgewood, Iowa.

Wash it all down with this tasty drink!

You will need:

- I can frozen cranberry juice concentrate
- I can frozen lemonade concentrate
- I liter lemon-lime soda
- I liter seltzer water
- frozen raspberries

Let cranberry juice and lemonade concentrates **thaw,** then mix with soda and seltzer in a punch bowl. **Add** some frozen raspberries and serve.

Lasagna Roll-Ups

E-mailed by Ashley M. of Birmingham, Alabama.

You will need:

- 2 cups ricotta cheese
- 1 cup grated mozzarella cheese
- 2 eggs, lightly beaten
- 8 ounces lasagna noodles, cooked (Cook these with an adult.)
- jar of pasta sauce

Ask an adult to help you **preheat** the oven to 350 degrees. **Mix** ricotta cheese, mozzarella cheese, and eggs. Take a lasagna noodle and **lay** it out. Spread some of the mixture over the noodle. Leave a little room on the ends and the sides of the noodle so that the cheese won't **ooze** out when you roll up the noodle. **Roll** the noodle. Place the noodle edge down in a baking dish coated with pasta sauce. Repeat until you have rolled up all the noodles. **Pour** sauce over the top. **Bake** in oven for 15 minutes. Use oven mitts to remove roll-ups from oven—the dish will be hot!

What do you snack on when you're hungry? Here's a look at what the ZOOM production staff **snacked** on during the course of the summer shoot:

992 slices of pizza
1890 bagels
120 ounces of cream cheese
792 ounces of sparkling water
642 gummy bears
496 gummy worms
280 sticks of gum
23 cans of beans
22 cans of whipped cream
324 Oreo cookies

zoinks!

Meet Isabella
At Her Family's Italian Restaurant

Q: How old are you and where do you live?
Isabella: I'm twelve years old, and I live in Waltham, Massachusetts.

Q: How did you become a waitress at such a young age?
Isabella: My family owns this Italian restaurant. I was around seven when I started working here. There's nobody working here except for family. My sister and I waitress. Occasionally my other sister comes out to help if we're really busy. My brothers cook and my dad is the main chef. I like waitressing best.

Q: Do you ever get tips?
Isabella: Sure, I do!

Q: Do you like working in a restaurant?
Isabella: I have lots of fun because I'm with my family and people I know. I look forward to seeing them every week. I know that there are other kids who don't work in a restaurant at age twelve or don't even have a job, but we have as many good times here as other people have at home. It's a lot of fun. It's all about family.

Isabella's dessert specialty is **chocolate mousse.** She makes it herself and says, "It's good stuff." Here's a simple version of chocolate mousse you might want to try.

You will need:

- 1 cup milk
- 12 ounces semisweet chocolate chips or other semisweet chocolate
- ½ cup sugar
- 3 eggs

Ask an adult to help you with this recipe.
Bring milk to a **boil** in a saucepan. Put chocolate, sugar, and eggs in a blender. Carefully **add** the boiling milk. **Blend** the mixture for about 30 seconds. Then pour the mixture into a large serving bowl or into individual dessert dishes. **Chill** for an hour or more. Add whipped cream before serving, if desired.

Delicious Deep-Dish Pizzas

Sent in by Lily P. of Albany, New York.

Here's a **joke** e-mailed to us by Brianna E:

What's a dog's favorite pizza topping?

Answer: Pupperoni!

You will need:

- muffin tin
- cooking spray
- frozen pizza dough
- tomato sauce
- any of your favorite pizza toppings: pepperoni, mushrooms, onions, etc.
- shredded cheese

Ask an adult to help you with the oven.

Preheat oven to 350 degrees. Spray the tin with cooking spray. **Flatten** a piece of dough and line each muffin cup. **Spread** sauce on top of the dough. Add toppings if you wish. **Sprinkle** with cheese. Bake for 15–20 minutes. Using an oven mitt and a fork, pop out the pizzas and **enjoy!**

Holy Guacamole!

(Guacamole is pronounced Gwa-ka-mo-lee.)

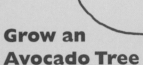

Ever tasted **rockin'** guac? Well, now's the time!

You will need:

- 2 ripe avocados (They're ripe when they're a little soft and their skins are almost black.)
- 4 teaspoons lemon juice
- 1 large plum tomato, chopped
- 1 tablespoon red onion, chopped
- a dash of salt and pepper
- corn chips, cucumber slices, or carrots for dipping

Ask an adult to help you **chop** the vegetables and peel the avocados. **Mash** the avocados. (Save at least one of the pits.) Mix in all the other ingredients. **Dip** chips or raw vegetables in your guacamole.

P.S. If you like, you can add 3 or 4 tablespoons of bottled salsa instead of the onion and tomato.

Grow an Avocado Tree

Don't throw that avocado pit away! You can grow an avocado plant with an avocado pit, 4 toothpicks, and a glass of water with a narrow mouth.

Wash the pit. **Stick** the toothpicks into the pit around its middle. **Set** the pit in a glass of water—the fat bottom of the pit should be underwater. The top of the pit will be dry. **Place** the glass in a sunny place. **Add** water when needed to keep the bottom of the pit wet. In about a week, you should see **roots** growing in the water. When your pit has grown two sets of leaves, **plant** it in soil in a sunny place. If you live in a warm climate, you can plant it outside; otherwise keep the plant **indoors** in a pot. Chances are that your tree won't bear fruit—and certainly not for many years—but you can **enjoy** a nice avocado plant!

P.S. You can also grow a sweet potato plant using this toothpick and glass technique.

Here's a joke from Brittney C. of Chicago, Illinois:

What did the alien say to the gardener?

Answer: Take me to your weeder.

47

Tasty Popcorn

Pep up your popcorn with these terrific toppings. Don't forget to pop in your favorite movie!

The recipes on these pages are variations of classic popcorn.

For **classic** popcorn, **you will need:**

- popcorn
- butter

optional: salt

Ask an adult to help you—popcorn can get **VERY HOT!**

Pop the popcorn according to the **instructions** on the package. Put about ¹/₂ stick of butter in a microwave-safe container and micro-wave it until it **melts** (about 45 seconds). Then **add** any of the toppings below and stir.

Taco Popcorn

Sent in by Steve M. of Clark, New Jersey.

Mix some taco seasoning into the melted butter. Add a little for a little **spice** or a lot if you like it really spicy. Pour it over the popcorn and stir. **Buen provecho!**

Toppings

Sugar and Spice Popcorn

E-mailed by Lauren E. of Richardson, Texas.

Add cinnamon and sugar (more sugar than cinnamon) to the melted butter. **Stir** a little to let the sugar dissolve. **Pour** over popcorn, mix, and enjoy.

Maple Popcorn

Sent in by Kathleen S. of Concord, Massachusetts.

Add maple syrup to the melted butter. Stir and pour over popcorn. Mix and **dig in!**

Z fact:

Every popcorn kernel contains some moisture. When the kernel is heated up, the **moisture expands,** causing the kernel to "pop" open.

Scrumptious Seven-Layer Dip

This dip is great for a party or any old time.

You will need:
- can of refried beans
- 8 ounces sour cream or plain yogurt
- diced onion
- jar of taco sauce
- shredded lettuce
- diced tomatoes or salsa
- shredded cheddar cheese
- tortilla chips for dipping

Ask an adult to help you chop the vegetables. Spread a layer of each of the first 7 ingredients in a shallow pan, starting at the top of the list. The final layer should be cheese. Use chips to scoop and eat the dip.

Sent in by Melissa W. of Sicklerville, New Jersey.

P.S. Add cooked shredded chicken or cooked ground beef if you like. But then you'll have to call it Eight-Layer Dip!

Here's a joke from Jamie G. of Hooksett, New Hampshire:

A cabbage, a tomato, and a sink had a race. How did it turn out?

Answer: The cabbage came out a head, the sink is still running, and the tomato is trying to catch up!

One-of-a-Kind Cupcake Cones

Sent in by Grace A. of Chelsea, Vermont.

Ubone ubof muby fubavuborubite thubings ubi dubid ubon Zuboom wubas mubakubing Cubupcubake Cubones. I lubove thubem!

You will need:
- any kind of cake mix and the ingredients listed on the box
- flat-bottomed ice cream cones
- any kind of frosting
- sprinkles or jimmies

Ask an adult to help you with the oven.

Preheat oven to 325 degrees. Prepare cake mix according to instructions. **Fill** each cone with cake batter until it is ³/₄ full. **Stand** the cones up on a pan. Bake for 10–15 minutes.

Let the cones **cool.** Then **frost** them and **dip** them into a shallow bowl of sprinkles or jimmies.

Fannee Doolee

loves **cooking** but hates **baking.** Why do you think that is?

51

Frozen "Watermelon"

Sent in by Jesska E. of Salt Lake City, Utah

You will need:

- large mixing bowl
- 1 quart lime sherbet
- 1 quart raspberry sherbet
- 12 ounces chocolate chips

This may look like a watermelon when you slice it, but it's 100% frozen sherbet!

Let the lime sherbet soften on the counter for a few minutes. Then **spread** it so it is a thick layer covering the inside of the mixing bowl. **Put** the bowl in the freezer until the lime sherbet hardens. Meanwhile, **let** the raspberry sherbet soften, then **stir** in the chocolate chips. When the lime sherbet is frozen, **take** the bowl out of the freezer and **fill** in the center with the raspberry sherbet mixture. **Freeze** the whole thing until it's hard. (This should take about 2 hours.)

Take your "watermelon" out of the freezer and **dip** the outside of the bowl in hot water. Then **turn** it over on a plate and remove the bowl. **Slice** and **serve** like watermelon.

Zfact:

A *citrullus lanatus* (that's the scientific name for watermelon) is 92% water.

You will need:

- 1 ½ cups semisweet chocolate chips
- smooth peanut butter
- mini-muffin tin lined with muffin wrappers

"I had fun making peanut butter cups. I love to cook at home, too—I can make a superb pecan pie."

Ask an adult to help you melt the chocolate chips in a microwave-safe bowl for 1 minute, stopping to **stir** the chips every 15 seconds. **Spread** a little chocolate in the bottom of each cup. Then **spoon** a layer of peanut butter into each cup. **Top off** each cup with more melted chocolate. **Put** the tin in the refrigerator until the peanut butter cups harden.

Peanut Butter Cups

Sent in by Evelyn M.

Zfacts:

The largest peanut butter factory in the world is in Ohio. It produces **250,000** jars of peanut butter a day.

Arachibutyrophobia is the fear of getting peanut butter stuck to the roof of your mouth.

No-Bake Cheesecake

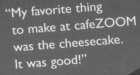

"My favorite thing to make at cafeZOOM was the cheesecake. It was good!"

You will need:

- 8 ounces cream cheese at room temperature
- 1 can sweetened condensed milk
- 1/3 cup lemon juice
- 1 teaspoon vanilla extract
- blender
- 1 store-bought graham cracker crumb piecrust

Ask an adult to help you use the blender.

Pour cream cheese, condensed milk, lemon juice, and vanilla in a blender. **Blend** until smooth. **Pour** mixture into the piecrust. **Refrigerate** for about 3 hours before serving.

P.S. Add fruit, like cherries or strawberries, to the top. Or make a Chocolate Marble Cheesecake—**use** a store-bought chocolate cookie piecrust and **swirl** some chocolate syrup into the mixture right before refrigerating.

Here's a joke from Stac of Oak Park, Illinois:

Where do hamburgers go to dance?

Answer: To a meatball

54

ZOOMa Cum Laude

Meet some kids who craft it, build it, and bake it — all for a good cause.

These ZOOMers have been awarded ZOOMa Cum Laude certificates in recognition of their outstanding contributions to their communities. We salute them and thank those who wrote in to nominate them!

ZOOMa Cum Laude

Chris O. of Jacksonville, Florida, volunteers for a group called Habitat for Humanity, which helps build houses for families who need them. Chris participated in a landscaping project, set out coolers at the construction site, and built a bench.

Build It!

Craft It!

ZOOMa Cum Laude

At the **Hillside, New Jersey Kids Café,** kids buy food and supplies and cook meals for kids who need them. Kids even make up the executive board, which approves all menus and field trips and manages the money for the café.

Bake It!

ZOOMa Cum Laude

Jacob H. of Columbia, South Carolina, set up a place at his school for people to recycle things like cereal boxes and old socks. Then he showed other kids how to make crafts and games out of them.

Everything You Always Wanted to Know About ZOOM

A Day in the Life of the ZOOMers

5:00 A.M. *Home.* We wake up, take showers, get dressed, eat breakfast, brush teeth, and head out the door for ZOOM.

8:05 A.M. *Makeup and wardrobe.* Since there are seven of us and only one of Sharon, the makeup artist, we take turns getting our makeup done and putting on our ZOOM clothes. When we are done, Jason and Arelitsa, the cast managers, take us to the ZOOMzone.

8:45 A.M. *ZOOMzone.* This is the place where we hang out when we are not on the set. The ZOOMzone is a big room filled with bean-bag chairs, games, crafts, and other cool things to do during downtime. Since it is our home away from home, we've also brought in some of our

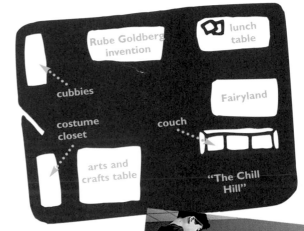

own stuff like posters, games, and stuffed animals. Here, Shea, the drama coach, leads us in a warm-up exercise. We do a different warm-up every day. One exercise we do is all hold hands in a circle and pass a pulse around by squeezing one another's hands.

9:00 A.M. *CafeZOOM.* We start taping. First up is Claudio, who leaves for the set to do a CafeZOOM segment. He is making Cupcake Cones. While he is on the set, Jenna, one of the associate producers, takes Kenny to another room so that he can learn how to make Kaleidoscopes for a ZOOMdo segment that is

being taped the next day. The rest of us work on this cool project that we started last week. We are building a fairy village out of sticks, leaves, dried flowers, and other stuff that we found outside. Caroline is making a neat-looking fairy swing out of an old tennis ball, some flowers, and some sticks.

9:45 A.M. *ZOOMzinger.* Claudio returns to the ZOOMzone and Jessie, Zoe, and Kenny leave for the set to do a ZOOMzinger. Since these are brainteasers, they have no idea what they are going to do ahead of time so that they don't guess the answer!

10:00 A.M. Chris, the science and math content manager, visits the ZOOMzone to work on an invention with Ray and Alisa. They are trying to build a machine that will put toothpaste on a toothbrush in twenty steps!

10:15 A.M. *ZOOMsci.* Caroline and Jessie head to the set to do a ZOOMsci segment. They are challenged to build a machine that will measure how much air their lungs can hold. While they're on the set, Shea

rehearses an Ubbi Dubbi scene with Ray and Alisa that will be taped later in the week.

11:30 A.M. *Zmail.* Jessie and Zoe are on the set to read a bunch of letters from the ZOOM hamper. It's always fun to see what people write!

12:00 P.M. *Lunchtime.* Everyone returns to the ZOOMzone, where lunch is waiting. Today we're eating Mexican food. We all put on smocks so we don't get food on our outfits. During lunch, Alisa teaches us this cool word game called "Contact."

12:45 P.M. Sharon, the makeup artist, visits us in the ZOOMzone to touch up our makeup and fix our hair.

1:00 P.M. *ZOOMchat.* We go to the set to chat about different topics that have been sent in by viewers. Zoe, Claudio, Jessie, Ray, and Alisa talk about moving. When we're not on camera, we spend time writing in our ZOOMjournals, which we got at the beginning of the season to record our experiences.

1:30 P.M. All of us ZOOMers are back in the ZOOMzone while the crew changes the set. Jason teaches us this really fun circle game called "This Is a Shoe."

1:45 P.M. *ZOOMsci.* Caroline, Kenny, Alisa, and Zoe are challenged to make boats out of Styrofoam trays, balloons, rubber

bands, and washers. Meanwhile, back in the ZOOMzone, Kenny, Ray, and Alisa goof off. They also play a game they invented called "Room-Shot." The object is to get a marble into a cup by rolling it across the room.

2:30 P.M. *Jokes.* We go to the set in pairs to do a bunch of jokes that have been sent in by viewers.

3:00 P.M. *ZOOMgames.* We all change into colorful T-shirts and head to the set to do a bunch of races, including a race where you have to walk with a large ball between your knees and one where you get into a sleeping bag and wriggle like an inchworm!

3:45 P.M. That's a wrap! We all head to wardrobe and change out of our outfits and back into our street clothes. Then we go and clean up the ZOOMzone. (Some days it can really be a mess!)

4:00 P.M. Our day is done! We head home.

Note: This schedule is actually an overview of several days. Typically we tape several segments of one kind in a row, like four CafeZOOMs.

Secret to Ubbi Dubbi
Revealed...

Hey, Ray.

Yeah, Caroline?

Just **add** the letters **"ub"** before every **vowel** sound and you, too, can speak Ubbi Dubbi. For instance, if your dog's name is Rover, he becomes Rubovuber. Got it? Grubeat!

Now **go** back and see if you can **read** the Ubbi Dubbi in this book — wube wubouldn't wubant yubou tubo **mubiss** ubout ubon ubanubythubing!

You can also **ubbify** your e-mail or **dubbify** notes to a friend in mere seconds by using the amazing Ubbi Dubbi translator on our Web site at **pbskids.org/zoom**

Dubid yubou hubave fubun rubeadubing thubis bubook?

Yubeah. Ubit mubakes mube wubant tubo gubo uband truby ubit uball ubout!

Who is Fannee Doolee?

There is a **pattern** to reading about Fannee Doolee. Fannee Doolee only **likes** things with **double** letters. Here's an example:

Fannee Doolee loves sweets but hates candy.

Notice how there are double letters, **"ee,"** in **"sweets"** but "candy" does **not** have any double letters. Why don't you try to write your own Fannee Doolee and send it to ZOOM!

The Old ZOOMers – Where Are They Now?

We asked the first-season ZOOMers to share their thoughts about life after ZOOM.

What was the best part of being on ZOOM?

Everyone agreed it was **meeting great people and hanging out** in the ZOOMzone between taping and rehearsing. Jared added that **lunch** was also one of his favorite things!

Last year, you spent the summer taping ZOOM. How did you spend this summer?

"This summer I **danced with a dance group.** We went to Disney for Magic Fun Day, and we danced at Camp Hill, Lauryn Hill's camp. I also work at a dance camp with members of our dance group." — **Lynese**

"This summer I **worked at a local repertory theater** as an assistant to all the employees." — **Pablo**

"This summer I **went to day camp.** I liked basketball, a game called Newcomb, and swimming. At the beginning of the summer, I went to an intense basketball camp for a week and lost five pounds from running around for five days straight! All the kids called me 'ZOOM.' I also acted in a community theater production." — **David**

"This summer I went on a **trip to Wyoming, Montana, Utah, and Colorado** and went hiking, white-water rafting, kayaking, and rock climbing. Then I baby-sat and went running and swimming with my friends." — **Keiko**

"This summer I was a **counselor at day camp.**" — Jared

Alisa and **Zoe** spent the summer doing the same thing they did last summer: working hard and having fun while **taping ZOOM.**

What do you want to be when you grow up, and have your ideas changed since ZOOM?

"Being on ZOOM showed me that not only do I want to become **an actor, but also a director, a cinematographer, a screenplay writer, and a producer.**" — Pablo

"I want to try to be a professional basketball player, but I think I might try acting and baseball, too." — David

"Now I don't want to be an actor. I want to be a doctor." — Keiko

"I want to be an actor even more now." — Jared

"I want to be a **police officer.**" — Lynese

"Since ZOOM, I've realized I want to direct, produce, and **other things besides act.**" — Alisa

"I want to do everything when I grow up, including travel, act, go into the Peace Corps, and help animals." — Zoe

"One of my favorite memories of ZOOM was singing the national anthem at Fenway Park with the other ZOOMers. The ball game was great that day, and I really had fun meeting all the ZOOM fans who came up to say hi to us in the stands." — David

Guess which ZOOMer said this! (Answers are at the bottom of the page.)

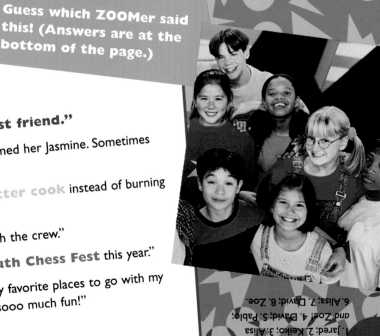

1. "I am **seven inches taller** than when I was on ZOOM!"

2. "I finally got my braces off!"

3. "On ZOOM I met **my best and closest friend.**"

4. "I got a sweet **new black kitten.** I named her Jasmine. Sometimes she sits on my shoulder like a parrot."

5. "The CafeZOOMs taught me to be a better cook instead of burning things."

6. "I loved **joking around** on the set with the crew."

7. "I came in **third in the Boston Youth Chess Fest** this year."

8. "I have to admit I **love to shop,** so my favorite places to go with my friends are to the mall and downtown. It's sooo much fun!"

Do you know how to make any cool crafts? Have you ever built anything? Do you have a favorite easy-to-make recipe? If you do, please e-mail us at www.pbskids.org/zoom or write to us at:

ZOOM
Box 350
Boston, Mass.
02134

If you **send** us your ideas,
you will receive a free issue of ZOOMerang,
and we might put **your** idea on the show!
All submissions become the property of ZOOM
and will be **eligible** for inclusion in all ZOOMmedia.
That means that we can **share**
your **ideas** with other ZOOMers on TV, on the Web,
in print materials, and in other ZOOM ways.

So, **c'mon** and send it to ZOOM!